DISCOURSE

GLOBAL LITERATURE MAGAZINE

(ISSUE #2_______Jan-June 2024)

<u>*ANTI-WAR POETRY NUMBER*</u>
Editor:
Aamir Abdullah

<u>PUBLISHER</u>

DISCOURSE I-SOL PULISHERS (PAKISTAN)

DISCOURSE

GLOBAL
LITERATURE
MAGAZINE
<u>*ANTI-WAR POETRY NUMBER*</u>

PUBLISHED BY:AAMIR SHAHZAD
Composing: Momina Aamir
Title:Momina Aamir
Layout &Design: Nisha Aamir
Printer:Kindle (Amazon)
CONTACT: +92 312 1703807
E-mail: discourseglmag@gmail.com

PREFACE

War, in its starkest form, leaves indelible scars on humanity, etching pain and loss into the hearts of countless individuals. In this special anti-war poetry edition of Discourse Global Literature Magazine, edited by Aamir Abdullah, a trilingual poet from Pakistan, we bring together voices from across the globe to speak out against the horrors of conflict. This bilingual collection, featuring poems in both English and Urdu, includes contributions from poets in Pakistan and fifteen other countries.

Through these powerful verses, our poets transcend borders and cultures, uniting in their call for peace and understanding. Each poem in this edition captures the profound anguish and futility of war, while also kindling a hope for a future where harmony prevails over hatred. By sharing these heartfelt expressions, we aim to foster a deeper appreciation for the sanctity of life and the universal desire for a world free from the ravages of war.

We invite you to journey through these pages, to listen to the poignant voices that resonate with a common plea for peace, and to join us in envisioning a world where the pen triumphs over the sword.

AAMIR ABDULLAH

Effects of Wars on the Natural Environment: (Free Verse in Urdu (1980 – Present) DR. MUHAMMAD IKRAM

TRANSLATED BY: AAMIR ABDULLAH

*T*he continuous advancement of science and technology has impacted every class and way of life. This progress has similarly affected the environment. Increasing urban populations, modern technology, transportation means, factory emissions, and waste have severely impacted the environment. Additionally, the devastating wars of the last century have led to significant resource wastage. Human activities have influenced the surroundings, or certain factors have occurred naturally, collectively affecting the environment.

The major powers of the world, filled with a sense of dominance and superiority, are prepared to engage in any activity, no matter how horrifying, to maintain their supremacy. They do not hesitate to play with nature. These global market forces are using scientists to create technologies and devices according to their desires, and the future of humanity—whether dark or bright—seems to lie in their hands. Dr. Zia-ul-Hasan writes:

"Scientists invent for them; technology experts create large machines for them, and the chemical substances from these industries pollute the underground water. We consume this poison without realizing that by doing so, we are inviting our own death. Underground nuclear explosions shake the earth; nuclear tests in the oceans devastate marine life, but since our immediate survival is not threatened, we remain silent and allow a handful of people to do as they please."

(Dr. Zia-ul-Hasan)

Since 1980, key themes in free verse poetry have included pollution, rising urban populations, women's issues, horror and terror, fear, anxiety, despair, and secularism. Among these, a significant theme revolves around the preservation of the natural environment, its degradation, love for animals, pollution, industrial development, and the damage caused by war activities. Our focus here will be on the damage to nature and the environment caused by wars or war activities and explosives.

Regarding nuclear devastation, many references can be found in the poems of Ali Muhammad Farshi. Hiroshima and Nagasaki are two Japanese cities where the United States dropped atomic bombs on August 6 and 9, 1945, during World War II. It is estimated that around 350,000 human lives were lost, and both cities were completely burned to ashes. It is said that even those who went to search for their loved ones after the bombings were killed by the radioactive rays. In this nuclear attack, all animals, plants, and insects were completely destroyed. It is said that even after 77 years, the effects of radiation are still present. A survivor named Hibakusha stated that on that day, everything in the city was reduced to ashes: people, birds, dragons, flies, grass—everything. Here are a few lines about nuclear devastation and the use of such weapons and their consequences. Poem of Ali M.Farshi:

With their magical hands, They tossed atomic bombs like balls. The spectators were astonished, How the magicians Turned the earth Into a handful of ash!

(Ali Muhammad Farshi)

In another poem, he writes: Whenever they desire, In the chambers of Mona Lisa and Venus, In the gardens where fairies and nymphs roam, They will create Hiroshima and Nagasaki, Unleashing the dance of death. (Ali Muhammad Farshi)

Terror, Explosives, Blasts, and Such Destruction:

A Hallmark of the Modern Era

Destructive elements use bombs, explosives, and blasts to instill fear and panic among people to achieve their nefarious objectives. These acts not only impact humans but also cause devastation to all living and non-living entities in the environment and nature. The earth cracks, greenery is destroyed, tree leaves fall, the air becomes polluted with smoke and the stench of explosives, buildings tremble far and wide, countless visible and invisible creatures perish in an instant, and those who survive are often left crippled or disabled, with only a fortunate few escaping unscathed. People involved in such activities do not adhere to any religion or faith. Religion has always been seen as a threat in the modern world, and hence, distant ties to religion are often used to link such events. However, it can be unequivocally stated that all religions in the world preach peace and love. If their followers misinterpret them or terrorists cloak themselves in the guise of religion, it is not the fault of the religions. Almost all religions in the world teach goodness and deter evil in their own ways.

In Naseer Ahmad Naser's poem "Cry of Death Between Dream and Sleep," a nighttime scene is depicted where darkness prevails all around. Suddenly, a blast occurs, and its light spreads instantly. The wind picks up, and the sound of the explosion is heard from afar. Observe the verse:Naseer Ahmed Nasir

Terror, Explosives, Blasts, and Such Destruction: A Hallmark of the Modern Era

When explosives detonate, there is a flash of light, which the poet refers to as "the moon appeared." The explosion not only pollutes the air but also affects every living being. Human conveniences have become widespread, modernized means of transportation have been developed, and vehicles and airplanes have been made for comfortable travel. Chemical weapons have been created for self-protection or to eliminate enemies. The experiments with these chemical weapons and their use on battlefields have polluted the atmosphere. Even today, in the on-going wars between Russia and Ukraine, and Palestine and Israel, human casualties are counted, but the birds, animals, insects, and other creatures are not taken into account. Naseer Ahmad Naser points out that these radioactive elements have started to dull the beautiful colors of nature. The butterflies that once had vibrant wings have now turned gray from the smoke and dust. Observe the verse:

"Radiation fires are burning Flowers are blackened by the ugly smoke, The wings of butterflies have turned grey."

(Naseer Ahmad Naser)

Due to deforestation and human chemical experiments, not only has the atmosphere become polluted, but there has also been a decrease in vapor and underground water. In recent decades, the underground water level has significantly dropped, water has become polluted, and the air is also contaminated. This pollution, mixing with our food and breath, has become the cause of various diseases. It is evident that the rate of illness has also significantly increased. Another poem by the same poet addresses the effects of reduced vapor and underground water on trees and the harmful impacts of radiation on human life. The poem reads:

"Neither is there rain-bearing clouds above, Nor is there life-sustaining water underground, The natural world has disappeared, The smile of vegetation has vanished, Radiation desires have flourished, Veins are crawling with sand-fish, snakes, and scorpions."

(Naseer Ahmad Naser)

Syed Mubarak Shah's poem "Alam Tarkif" from his collection "Jungle Guman" (Imaginary Forest) makes a plea to the Almighty, similar to how Allah sent birds to destroy the invaders of Mecca. He compares today's oppressors to Abraha, who is devastating cities, burning people's homes, and birds' nests. Observe the verse:

"O solitary resident of the timeless abode, When someone came to destroy Your house, The birds became messengers of death, And in my country, All the inhabited houses burned down, And the birds' nests all burned."

(Syed Mubarak Shah)

Abraha, the king of Abyssinia, a Christian by faith, attacked Mecca in 570 AD with the intention of demolishing the Kaaba and constructing a central church for Christians there. His army included elephants, which is why that year is also known as the Year of the Elephant in Arab history. When Abraha attacked, Allah sent flocks of birds carrying stones in their claws. These birds dropped the stones, which caused the bodies of the soldiers and animals they hit to burst, leading to their painful deaths. The poet references this historical event, lamenting to God that when His house was attacked, birds came as angels of death to save it. However, in his own country, modern-day Abrahas are burning houses, including birds' nests. He beseeches God to empower the birds today as He did before to protect themselves and his homeland. Essentially, the poet is complaining to God, asking Him to empower the elements of nature to fight against oppressive forces, just as He empowered the birds to save His house. This is a plea for divine intervention to protect the weak and the natural world from the destructive forces of modern-day oppressors. Wars are fought by humans for their objectives. Regardless of the basis of these wars, nature remains entirely innocent. No matter the scale of human casualties, the damage to nature and the environment is far greater. Insects, birds, animals, trees, plants, and greenery suffer, and the air becomes polluted, carrying diseases wherever it flows. In regions where bombs and explosives rain down, life cannot return to normal for a long time. Hiroshima and Nagasaki have become proverbial examples in this regard. Pakistan and India have been adversaries for a long time, with their armies constantly stationed at the border. These two nations have gained global notoriety as traditional rivals and enemies. Both sides continuously exchange fire. While human casualties are counted, the environmental destruction is often overlooked. Trees, birds, insects, land, water, and natural beauty are being ravaged by human activities and mutual animosities. It is even more regrettable that this devastation is rarely mentioned. A few sympathetic poets express this concern in their verses.

The continuity of this theme is found in the poem "Ababeels are Captive," where the poet conveys that the oppressors, whom God once destroyed, have now not only conquered the world but also the cities that were once protected. These oppressors have even enslaved the birds, who now only sing their names. Here, the poet presents the birds as symbols of resistance, who would come to aid the oppressed at any moment.

Syed Mubarak Shah's poem "Hadaf" addresses the pollution of the atmosphere caused by nuclear devastation, leading to the death and disability of birds and humans. It sends a message to the oppressors that one day the same polluted air will claim the lives of the predatory beasts. During general wars, it is observed that invading soldiers not only ravage human life but also hunt birds in the forests. The poet draws attention to this issue as follows:

"But what is this strategy during these campaigns That you kill and capture the flying birds in the forest And in the settlements, You capture and kill them?" (Syed Mubarak Shah)

The poet suggests that the responsibility for the death of birds or humans who have become paralyzed or whose limbs have failed, or who have been killed in attacks, falls on everyone. Remember, this game of fire and explosives will take everyone's life. Air and wind cannot be confined by national borders. In the historical context of the subcontinent, during their dominance, the British hunted countless wild animals and forced people to grow crops that would yield the highest agricultural exchange. The Bengal famine was a consequence of this.

Humans have always had a deep connection with nature. Like other animals, they lived a natural life. Standing upright distinguished humans from other animals. Their structure allowed them to stand for long periods and see far distances. Their hands and bodies were such that they could easily create tools. Their cognitive abilities were superior to other animals. Thus, humans began to differentiate themselves. They made weapons, created comfortable sleeping places, wore clothes, organized into groups to hunt other animals, and enjoyed culinary delights by cooking meat. They tamed animals, developed transportation, and continued the journey of civilization; today, they reach for the sky, create artificial rain, and employ chemical methods for thunder and lightning, forgetting that there have always been set boundaries for their actions, which ensure their safety.

<u>Ravash Nadeem writes:</u>

"Listen friends! Until yesterday, Humans used to swing on green tree branches, But when they learned to stand on their hind legs, They took axes in their hands. Now it is heard that they make gun handles from their temples."

Once, humans worshipped natural phenomena, such as the moon, sun, snakes, bulls, and trees. But today, the same humans are cutting down the trees they once worshipped. Nature remains silent, enduring all pain and suffering quietly. The poem "Soil, You Have Magic" reminds the reader of the nature and wonders of the earth. Aamir Abdullah draws our attention to the marvels of soil:

It purifies muddy water, revitalizes everything when it burns, sustains life, and makes every scene lush and green. The poet speaks of the qualities of soil:

"From your silence, Words were born. Every scene was created from your eye, And deep, unique colors were filled."

Here, the poet refers to the creation of Adam from soil, giving birth to life in the universe. The earth shapes every scene and beautifies its surroundings. Beautiful greenery and lush colors are all created from it. After highlighting the importance of soil, the poet talks about the injustices inflicted upon it by humans:

"Soil, for ages, Endures the test of fire, Swallows the flames of pain, Yet never utters a cry or sigh, Keeping every wound on its chest hidden."

Nature endures all oppression and cruelty in silence, while humans continue their domination and tyranny. If we see "soil" as a symbol in this poem, it embodies the same virtues as a mother. Any mother who feeds her children turns ordinary water into nectar. She teaches them to speak, continuing the process of evolution. She bears all pain quietly. Giving importance to nature and considering natural entities as alive and equal to humans is a key tenet of ecological criticism. This theory advocates living and letting live, asserting that everything and everyone is important. "Nothing is insignificant in nature's factory" is its premise, opposing any notion of superiority.

Irfan Shahood's love for nature is ingrained in him. In the poem "Before the War," he wrote to a friend in India as tensions rose on the Pakistan-India border, praying for the preservation of natural elements amid human conflict. In wars, countless precious gifts of nature and natural phenomena face destruction, beyond measure. Hiroshima and Nagasaki are examples that history can never forget Seventy-two years have passed since the American atomic bombing of the Japanese city of Nagasaki. During World War II, the United States dropped atomic bombs on Hiroshima and Nagasaki. These two historic atomic attacks on Japan claimed the lives of over two hundred thousand people, with double that number affected by radiation. The attack on Nagasaki occurred on August 9, 1945, when a B-29 aircraft dropped an atomic bomb code-named "Fat Man." This bomb wreaked havoc in Nagasaki, killing approximately seventy thousand people according to Japanese records, including twenty-three to twenty-eight thousand Japanese aid workers and a large number of forced laborers of Korean descent.

Wars cause significant damage to the natural environment, a fact deeply felt by Irfan Shahood, who incorporates this awareness into his poetry. In a poem, while offering prayers for the inhabitants of an enemy country, he mentions various natural elements, including vegetation:

"May your trees play with sharks, be safe May squirrels also be safe in your acacia trees May our butterflies find life in the branch of light May all the paths of crops be everlasting, be safe"

<u>(Irfan Shahood)</u>

The poet understands how nuclear power can destroy entire settlements in an instant, with Hiroshima and Nagasaki as vivid examples. While these events occurred nearly eighty years ago, destructive capabilities have advanced significantly since then. Regarding Hiroshima and Nagasaki, Dr. Sophia Khushk writes:

"During the Second World War (1939-1945), the use of atomic bombs on Hiroshima and Nagasaki instantly killed millions and forced countless others to live a life of suffering. The effects of the bomb's radiation can still be seen today. Despite this, driven by a lust for power, humans successfully tested the neutron bomb in 1962 and created millions of deadly weapons, including the hydrogen bomb as a second-generation atomic bomb. In this context, ecological criticism emerged"

(Dr. Sophia Khushk).

In another poem, Irfan Shahood prays for the protection of neighborhoods, villages, fields, trees, and plants from all kinds of destruction. He wishes for flowers to bloom and fruits to grow on these trees, and for birds to come and sing on them. Here are a few lines from the poem: "My dear, May your land and your neighborhood remain spacious May all the streets of your planet be lively May the green fragrance remain in your fields May the newly blossomed flowers sing on your trees May the songs of birds make you sing" (Irfan Shahood)

Irfan Shahood has adopted a resistance tone in his poetry, becoming a shield for the weak. Nature endures all oppression silently, but it is the duty of humans to protect it from destruction. In his poetry, Shahood complains to God about those who have damaged the natural environment. Here is an excerpt:

"If one day I meet God on the road, I will tell Him About the one who stole the green beauty of the lands, And the one who had the squirrels' trees cut with saws, And the one who trapped birds in electric waves"

(Irfan Shahood)

Since time immemorial, humans have used various tactics to suppress weaker voices and assert their dominance. Occasionally, elements of nature resist this behavior. Irfan Shahood's poetry is drawn to these resisting voices. His poems suggest that he advocates for the voiceless, incorporating their struggles into his work.

Since the partition of India, Kashmir has been a region of unrest and turmoil. The condition in occupied Kashmir is particularly distressing, with daily curfews and gunfire ruining the atmosphere. The poet captures this tragic situation in his poem "Kashmir." The neutral opinion is that the beautiful region of Kashmir is being devastated by the ongoing conflict between Pakistan and India, with both countries using it as a battlefield. Here are a few lines from the poem:

"Heavenly angels, Create harmony For shrouds now hang from the apple trees The fruitful crown of the trees is touching the ground The rivers are flowing with the filth of sorrow"

<u>(Irfan Shahood)</u>

Kashmir's forests are rich in wild apples, and the land is highly suitable for apple cultivation. In this poem, the poet explains that due to explosives, bombs, and bullets, the apple trees in Kashmir are now barren. Often, disruptive elements cut down apple trees to weaken the local economy. The use of weapons and explosives in the conflict between Pakistan and India has become a daily occurrence. Both countries have fought wars over Kashmir but remain steadfast in their positions, with the most significant impact being the destruction of the natural environment.

DR. RATAN GHOSH (INDIA)

Dr. Ratan Ghosh, *a luminary in the realm of Bharatiya Bi-Lingual literature, stands as a distinguished addition to the Advisory Board of Panorama International Literature Festival (PILF) 2024. A passionate and prolific author, editor, and academician, Dr. Ghosh has left an indelible mark on the literary landscape. His creative expressions, spanning various genres, have garnered acclaim not only nationally but across the globe.*

Dr. Ghosh's poetic prowess has found its way into numerous esteemed platforms, including

National and International E-journals, journals, magazines, and paperback anthologies. His literary contributions are diverse, reflecting a deep engagement with various facets of the human experience.

Dr. Ghosh's poems have been transliterated into many languages. Dr. Ghosh is well known as the co-editor of an International Journal titled "The Mirror of Time". He has created, recreated and defined a different literary genre. His short stories illuminate human psyche connecting past, present and future of every individual. His novels represent him and the society he lives in. They are the testimony of time and space reflecting unforgettable history of his forefathers.

His significant literary works include captivating titles such as "Bra And Other Tales," "The Memoirs Of A Forlorn Man," "Footprints: Voices of Refugees," "The Weeping Soul," "My Love," and "Quotable Quotes." Each piece adds a unique hue to the literary canvas, showcasing the versatility and depth of Dr. Ratan Ghosh's literary repertoire.

Dr. Ratan Ghosh, a luminary in the realm of Bharatiya Bi-Lingual literature, stands as a distinguished addition to the Advisory Board of Panorama International Literature Festival (PILF) 2024. A passionate and prolific author, editor, and academician, Dr. Ghosh has left an indelible mark on the literary landscape. His creative expressions, spanning various genres, have garnered acclaim not only nationally but across the globe.

*** * ***

EAST

Just a few decades walked away!

Just a few decades!
From the garden of my heart
When my backbone was buried
In the bed of Padma I wept a lot!
I wept while walking away from my bed like a thief
But my heart was robbed
While I felt my dripping sobs
Dripping by my cheeks
While I was crossing the river of the East
Which was streaming the blood stream
I wanted to bush again the vibes of my saddened past
To get back the snow of the lost
But...!
I stood up
And fell
Stood up
And fell
Stood up
And fell
Again and again like a handicapped beggar
To cherish another garden in the bush under Western sky
Neither the garden nor the snow I felt, sprouting
When I feel the fragrance of my blood streams
Left years before
In the burial of bloodshed and rape
I walk again and again
To bush my garden
But I feel my sobs -

Falling upon my hope...!
Falling upon my hope ...!
* * *

ANIL KUMAR PANDAY (INDIA)

Anil Kumar Panday was born in a small town, Brajrajnagar, in the state of Odisha, India. He has already published two books of poetry namely- Fragrance of Love and Melody Of Love. His poems have been published in many national and International anthologies and e-magazines. Themes of his poems are mostly romance and nature. Currently he is working on his third book. He takes interest in travelling and meeting people.

***

Page |

19

TITLE: SOMEDAY THE WAR WILL END

*Someday from the edge of the
Horizon a fresh wind will blow
There will be a new sun in the sky to
Shine and make the hills and valleys to glow
Someday the poisoned dusts
Of the cannons will settle down
There will be no sound of guns and
Peace and love will return to our town
Someday mothers will get back
Their sons and fathers will go to work
Prayers will be sung in the mosques, temples
And churches and clouds will not remain dark
Someday children will come out
Smiling into the streets and dance and play
Fresh flowers will bloom all around
Dew drops will shine on grasses and hay
The war will end for sure
People will come together to share love
A world of joy will thrive under
The blue sky and He will bless us from above*

* * *

CHAD NORMAN(CANADA)

T

he Poet Francesco Favetta was born in the land of Sicily in Sciacca, he has always loved poetry, writing verses, but above all culture, food for the soul: culture is Freedom, it is Free Spirit, it is Soul in Motion, not should never be harnessed!

In 2018 he was awarded the Academician of Sicily by the Accademia di Sicilia.

He has been published in various anthologies and magazines, among which we mention a few:

international magazine The Poet;

Revista Azahar which edited the first anthology of poems in Spanish: Encantamiento y Palabras como Plumas;

Anthology The Silk Road Anthology: Nano Poems for Africa; "Poetic Galaxy Atunis";

WorldSmith International Editorial; OPA The Poetry Journal; Innombrable magazine; Polis Magazine; rank of minister in the Order of the Titan and publication of a lyric in Octobermania;

international literary magazine Kavya Kishor in Bangladesh;

international magazine of language, literature and culture "Petrushka Nastamba" Serbia; international magazine, Namaste India and certificate of appreciation;

Different Truths social journalism platform;

Cisne Revista Digital;

Humanity magazine St. Petersburg; fourth Panorama International Literature Festival Spain, delegate for Italy.
He founded a theater company in Sciacca: "Theatrum Socialis Sciacca", and a Lions Club, "Sciacca Terme".
Finally, the Poet Francesco Favetta is convinced that Poetry will be the weapon with which humanity will set its life free, and furthermore that Beauty will always be a truth, which will never be buried:
from the times and events of daily human life!

* * *

SORRY HUMANITY!

*Children killed
in the silence of the world
tortured women
grieving mothers
blood on the streets
a red river
that screams pain
dissolved in the earth
still wet with death
of innocence severed.
Sorry humanity
we are the victims
forget
we are the souls
homeless
we are the burden
on consciences
unshed tears
rights denied
we are the stolen life.*

WE ARE PALESTINIAN CHILDREN
*They are children
far away
they are invisible
they don't weigh on the heart
but in silence they die
without awakening
anger*

riots
or vomiting
retching and stomach ache.
They do not count
Nothing
I am not meat
they are not blood
they are only Palestinians
nobody's children
servants without a country
souls robbed of life
murdered hearts
they are cannon fodder.
IN THE ROOTS OF THE HEART!
Far from life
away from everything
in the silence of the earth
in hidden places
to human eyes
where the time
is suspended
lives in the rock
in the roots of the heart
the voice always on
of pure love
UNWORTHY CRIMINAL MAN !
I saw you
was you
the heartless face
black soul
criminal man
slave of evil

cruel killer.
Endless abyss
you are a dark well
your smile is poison
your every speech
it's a screamed lie
unworthy to be
you are a slothful beast.

SON OF FREEDOM

Another day
it's not a dark night
maybe life will change
but we will never see
fall into doubt
the son of freedom.
He still reigns in the world
the wolf's robe
and has human features
it's the evil behind the wall
he is the man without a heart
the modern brute animal.

IT'S LIKE THE WIND !

Rooted in silence
the warrior's heart beats
rushes like trains
they march in his blood
it's a rock
because it doesn't chip
his animal is fire.
In his eyes
burns eternally

the passion for life
gear
with light footsteps
to destiny
it never meets.
It's like the wind
fly up and forward
captures every moment
the pure breath of beauty
it goes higher and higher
it only goes down when
love is present.

* * *

DIMITRIS P. KRANIOTIS

(Greece)

Dmitris P. Kraniotis was born in 1966 in Larissa Prefecture in central Greece and he grew up in Stomio (Larissa). He studied Medicine at the Aristotle University of Thessaloniki. He lives in Larissa (Greece) and works as a medical doctor (internal medicine specialist physician). He is the author of 10 poetry books in Greece and abroad.He has won international awards for his poetry which has been translated in 35 languages. He participated in several International Poetry Festivals around the World.He is Doctor of Literature,Academician in Italy, President of the 22nd World Congress of Poets(UPLI), President of the World Poets Society (WPS), Director of the Mediterranean Poetry Festival (Larissa, Greece), Chairman of the Writers for Peace Committee of PEN Greeceand member of several organizations: World Poetry Movement (WPM), Poets of the Planet (PoP), Hellenic Literary Society, National Society of Greek Literary Writers, etc.

***

ODE TO THE PEACE HERO

You were born once
For a thousand revolutions
You died once
With a thousand resurrections
You enlightened eternal ideals

Into chests full of dreams
You blew poets' words
Into harmonious winds
You got hurt by faceless wounds
And slapped injustices
You fought for freedom
And won for peace

* * *

TAPAS DAY (India)

I'm Tapas Dey, living at Mathabhanga, West Bengal, ndia and a teacher by profession and an evid reader of poetry and poetry writing is my passion.My many poems have already been included in Prodigy Magazine, USA, Humanity Magazine, Russia, ILA magazine USA, Hyperpoem, Russia, The best of 2020 and The best of 2022, USA, Paradise on earth, Vol.1&2 USA, Over the rainbow, Greece, Polis free press, Litterateur Rw, India and many more.

***

THE MESSAGE, 'NO WAR'

From the sky,
A shower of rain is on my two eyes,
From the eyes,
Line of stream is running down my cheeks.
In a palette,
I collect till the last drop of water.
Somebody tells me,
Don't mix black ink with water
To write a fancy tale,
Mix white colour with it,
Draw a white pigeon and
Let it fly in the sky and announce
The message, ' No war.'
No war, only echoing everywhere 'No war

***

FROSINA TASEVSKA (Macedonia)

Frosina Tasevska was born in the Republic of Macedonia. She is a bilingual poet and writer. She writes in English and Macedonian languages. She has authored two solo poetry collections. She is an active member of various literary and creative platforms. Her writings are part of several national and international magazines, newspapers, journals, and anthologies. She has won many awards for her write-ups. She holds the degrees of B.Ed. (English) and currently, works as an educator.

* * *

ENOUGH

Today's reality is war.
The selfish world we live in today.
War ragged, faces dirt-encrusted, black.
The blood in the streets.
Sophisticated weapons
generate a war-like dance.
Missiles armed with warheads
are poised from a distance.
War. War. War!
No one knows, what it's for.
Fight because you're told to
or because you think it's right.
Blanched skulls and bones.

Pain, riot, bombardment
And one graveyard.
Enough death, enough sorrow, end war!
** * **

EDY SAMUDRA
KERTAGAMA(Indonesia)

Edy samudra Kertagama: As a director and poet, he has released solo anthologies such as Mantra Sang Nabi, Carriage Hand in Hand, and Poem of the Rajawali Bird, as well as Nyanyian Sunyi dan Kering (all of which are archived in the Dutch Laeden library). Poems published in regional, national, and international media, including an anthology with 39 world poets. His works in manuscript: Madah Nyai Rossina, Laila Love In the House I Built (both long poems), The House I Built, are included in the anthology THE MIST, which features 20 international writers. His poems have appeared in 60 anthologies released by both Indonesian and foreign writers. Send an email to edysamudrakertagama@yahoo.co.id.
** * **

A PIECE OF THE MOON IS MISSING
By : Edy Samudra Kertagama

Let go of any current disagreements, allow everything to return to its natural state, and then don't sharpen the machete; instead, save it for us to use to cut down the weeds so we can sow seeds there. And later, when it's Panin time, we immediately celebrate by letting go of all the tightness in our chests, for what we call mother is our hometown, and father is a house on stilts for us and those born from the same womb to seek shelter in.

We don't need to go back in time since all of the fairy tales we've heard were engraved long ago on dark stone walls, and we must not ignore them, even if it means being driven away by wind, rain, and storms.

If amid the leaves, twigs, and roots that stretch into the earth are the eyes of a thousand dreams that always yearn to meet Him at night so that all the previous melancholy would return to become a flower held by the wanderer, then everyone can take notes.

So, if we really want to hug Him, let's say hello to Him, even if it's just a shard of the moon that landed on a rock as we were reminiscing about the past, as we let go of all the arrogance that has been sitting in our hearts for a long time.

* * *

EVA LIANOU PETROPOULOU(GREECE)

She *is an awarded author and poet from Greece with more than 25 years in the Literary field published more that 10 books.*

Her poems are translated in more than 15 languages. She is President of creativity and art of Mil Mentes Por Mexico Association represent Greece, President of Global UHE Peru, Vice President of Cultural Association China, Mexico.

***

PEACE

Peace,
So expensive
We buy so many weapons
To maintain it
If we pray more
If we were kind to each other
We could say
We have Peace of mind
Poetic heart
Call for meditation
Inside our heart
Peace,
We say a lot

We make nothing
Peace,
Such as a woman
We adore
But few can get
Peace,
A value with no cost
If the humans understand the word...
I wish one day....

* * *

ASHOK CHAKRAVARTHY
THOLANA (INDIA)

Ashok Chakravarthy Tholana is a writer-poet-reviewer, hailing from Hyderabad City, Telangana State, INDIA, whose message-oriented poems achieved a rare distinction of getting published in no less than a hundred countries. His relentlessly contributions on Universal Peace, World Brotherhood, Environment Consciousness, Protection of Nature, Safeguarding Children's and Human Rights; the poet has been conferred with several prestigious national and international awards, lots of laurels, commendations, titles and notably TEN doctorates. That apart, his poems have been translated into 40 languages as of now. Ashok received applause from Dr. APJ Abdul Kalam, former-President, India, Shri Atal Behari Vajpayee, former-Prime Minister, India, Bill Clinton, USA, Queen Elizabeth of Britain, Princess of Wales, President and Prime Minister of France, Prime Minister of Switzerland, Senator Viktor

Busa, The Lord President, Italy, United Nationals Organization,

UNESCO, UNICEF etc.

Ashok Chakravarthy Tholana
Poet-Writer-Reviewer, INDIA
Cell: +91 9866524363

CHEN HSIU-CHEN ???

PEOPLE AND GOD 

The people on both sides of the war
Believe the same God.
The left side insists——the truth is ours,
The right side insists——the justice is ours.
Both sides face toward the same God at same time
to pray for the victory on the same battlefield.
The God is separated into two halves
and caught in a dilemma.
The people on both sides of the war
believe different Gods.
Both sides face toward own God to pray
for the victory on the same battlefield.
The left side insists own to be victory,
The right side insists opposite to be defeated.
The war between people and people
becomes an innocent war
between God and God.
The people utilizes missiles to decide
whose God
is a real one.

VICTOR EMMANUEL IKPONWOSA(NIGERIA)

Victor Emmanuel Ikponwosa also known as Sir write man is a young Nigerian poet, writer and blogger. Victor has been writing for more than five years. He hasn't published any of his works but he has been sharing them on social media platforms.

Victor has won numerous accolades and certificates from online poetry forums for his beautifully crafted poems.

He studied literature for three years at Air Force Comprehensive School, yola, Nigeria and emerged as the best literature Student during his time.

Victor loves writing poetry during his spare time.

Victor strongly believes that words have the capacity to create a better society and cause positive reforms.

On Fri, Dec 29, 2023, 8:54 AM Aamir Shahzad <discourseglmag@gmail.com> wrote:

Thanks for the submission.

Picture, short bio and Country name missing.

On Mon, Dec 25, 2023, 1:21 AM Sir write Man <sirwriteman@gmail.com> wrote:

***

THROWBACK BY E I VICTOR

I decided to look back
So I flashed back
And I was taken aback
I remembered how I survived the attack
The past was indeed black
I suffered a lot of flack
I was considered a hack
I was in lack
I lived in a shack
They said I was a drawback
I had no greenback
I looked like a maniac
I had nothing but a rucksack
It was indeed a time of setback
But now , I'm a crackerjack
I made them rollback
My life is now on track
* * *

RAFIQ SANDEELVI(PAKISTAN)

HOW IS THE CLAMP

On which electro flying steed
are tightening saddles
For which of the combat
you intend again
For which course of the wild dream
is opened in your veins
The intention to fix a blood dripping flag
on the city walls
Again the longing to see
lacs of the conquered bodies weeping
in the state of chest beating
With which water of madness
are filling the pitcher of the ego
Listen! You are taking decision
in the mist of very ugly night
On that side
At the distance of hundreds miles
There is a hill
on the back of it
ignis fatuus are capering
leaping and jumping
Bushes full of leaves

walk on their feet
whirlwinds in the shape of balls
keep rolling
Dragon and porpoise
opening their mouth
come towards the slope
A world of black g...
*****

MUNAVVAR BOLTAYEVA
(Uzbekistan)

Hello. I am from Uzbekistan. I want to learn all world languages. I sent my poem in Urdu because I am interested in languages. I am learning this language.
<munavvar97boltayeva@gmail.com> wrote:

...سمندری پھول

ایک باصلاحیت فنکار کا کام،

ایک نایاب پھول، ایک خوبصورت پھول، ایک شاندار پھول۔

کیا پانی پھولوں کا رنگ نہیں دھوتا؟

ایک پھول جو سمندر کی تہہ سے نیلا اگتا ہے۔

یہ کسی دوسرے پھول کی طرح زندہ نہیں رہتا

...سمندر سے محبت کرنے والے دن رات

بگلے ہمیشہ بہاؤ کے ساتھ جاتے ہیں۔

...اگر تم اس سے محبت کرتے ہو

سمندر کے پھول، آپ کے پاس بہت سے راز ہیں،

کیا تم نے سمندر کا راز چھپایا؟

کیونکہ تم بہت خوبصورت ہو؟

آپ کی چادر میں کیا چھپا ہے؟

میں نے آپ کو ایک گانا لکھا، میں نے آپ کو ایک نظم لکھی۔

فنکاروں نے آپ کو دل سے کھینچ لیا۔

کبھی سمندر کے صبر کا امتحان لینے کے لیے

معذرت، انہوں نے جان بوجھ کر آپ کا امن توڑ دیا۔

آپ ایک محفوظ معجزہ ہیں۔

یہ بتاؤ تم نے یہ خوبصورتی کہاں سے حاصل کی؟

اے سمندر کے پھول، میں نے تمہیں گایا ہے۔
میں کتنا ہی گاتا ہوں، آیت کبھی ختم نہیں ہوتی۔
منور بولتائیفا

...چلنا

زندگی کی کشتی پر خواب دیکھنا۔
کبھی ہم دائیں، کبھی بائیں طرف تیرتے ہیں۔
تاکہ بدتمیز لہریں نہ ملیں،
کبھی کبھی ہم خاموشی کا دور توڑ دیتے ہیں۔
کتنے بچپن گزرے اس جہاز پر
کتنے سحر، کتنے دن ڈوب گئے۔
اگر کسی نے صبح نہیں دیکھی تو...
کچھ سورج کی وجہ سے جاگ گئے تھے۔
زندگی ہے اور صرف چلنا ہے۔
ایک جگہ پھنسنا نہیں ہے، ایک لمحے کے لیے بھی رکنا نہیں ہے۔
زمین بھی حرکت میں ہے، وقت کا کیا ہوگا؟ وہ جلدی میں ہے۔
گولی جیسے کسی شخص کا پیچھا کر رہی ہو...
اور پتہ صاف ہے۔ سبز تلسی۔
وہاں کی ندی میں رس بہتا ہے۔
لامتناہی پھلوں کے ساتھ بہت سے درخت ہیں۔
کھاوت ہے، نہ بارش ہوتی ہے نہ برف۔
نیلے رنگ کا چاند بھی ایک لمحے کے لیے نہیں رکتا
آخر اس کا بھی ایک خاص طریقہ ہے۔
لوگوں سے سننے کے لیے،
رات کو وہ ایک ایک کر کے آسمان پر نمودار ہوتے ہیں۔
زندگی کی کشتی میں ہم اب بھی سوار ہیں
ہمیں نہ ڈرا، جھوٹے سراب۔
صرف نیکی کو ہمارے ساتھی ہونے دو
ویسے بھی اس سڑک پر ہمارا برا حال ہے...
منور بولتائیفا

بولتائیفا منور کی عمر 27 سال ہے۔ سورکھندریہ، جمہوریہ ازبکستان۔ ان کی نظمیں 5 شعری کتابوں، 7 بین الاقوامی انتھالوجیز، امریکہ، ارجنٹائن، مصر، ایکواڈور، بلغاریہ، بھارت، چین، برطانیہ، انڈونیشیا، کولمبیا، اسپین،

ملائیشیا، ترکی، کوریا، سنگاپور میں شائع ہو چکی ہیں۔ بین الاقوامی سطح کے رضاکار۔ 90 سے زیادہ بین الاقوامی کانفرنسوں کے شریک۔ 50 سے "*Poética Universal Filial Uzbekistan*" زائد بین الاقوامی سطح کے سفیر۔ ایوارڈ کی فاتح۔ "*WIO GLOBAL WOMEN AWARD 2023*" نائب صدر۔ ازبکستان میں وائیو گلوبل ویمن ایوارڈ اکیڈمی کی سفیر۔ مائیٹی پینس ایوارڈ 2023 کا

***

ANWER RAHEEM (Pakistan)

LOVE POETRY FOR PEACE
NO TO WAR

Human born by the will of the creator perfectly
We are sons and daughters of Adam and Eve truly
We are black brown and white naturally
Color of our blood is red exactly
Gifted with beautiful Earth perfectly
Blessings and bounties we cannot deny obviously
Why we fight wars no reason is seen logically
Conduct dealings amongst all with sincerity
We can live together with true reality of humility
Our acts with one another be with serenity
More humane by enhancing our relations from sympathy to higher
limits of empathy
Live in this world with due tranquility
Welcome each other with hospitality
Respect liberty equality and enjoy fraternity
Have love peace faith hope with secure life for humanity
Stand determined for noble cause of peace unflinchingly
These character traits we all have received in scriptures divinely

***

SHAHID ABBAS (PAKISTAN)

Shahid Abbas is a multi-awarded International Author and Poet from Karapla 421 G.B, Tandlianwala Faisalabad Pakistan. He is the author of "Words from Nature" and the co-author of "We Speak In Syllables".

BELOVED RAIN

Today, you are pouring on my heart
I remain alone, but then you arrived and behaved like a soul part
I'm in love with you since the day
When you washed my sorrows and I had no words to say.
You are the beauty of the all beauties which rebirth the wonders
I never move to any trees under
Come what may, we love each other,
Thus no need to look for another
I can't hide my emotions as my eyes get wet,
When your drops pour on me as I sit
You are my beloved,
I remember the day when someone shoved
And I found myself among the heavenly drops
Wow, the love at first sight after the meeting I never stop
You and I are loyal friends

We adore each other and never offends
You are my everlasting crave
In your accompany, I wish to make a long drive
You are the cause of happiness for all creatures,
You inhale the beauty of all nature
Since the night I waited for you as I
gaze at the sky,
I talked about you to a pretty tiny sparrow, she smile and reply
Oh, Divine lover
I don't fly high
But I have been told a secret by one who never lies
Your beloved is coming through the heavenly door
So there is no need to wait for more.
***

TAGHRID BOU MERHI (Lebanon)

< taghrid240@gmail.com >

A PLEA FOR PEACE

In stanzas bold, the verses rise,
A tapestry of truth in poetic guise.
Antiwar Poetry, the sincere poetry,
A solemn decree, free with clear letter.
Verse by verse, a plea for peace,
Each syllable a call to cease.
Sonnets echo the pain and sorrows,
In every line, a plea to refrain.
Against the drums of conflict's beat,
These words arise, with strength and hope.
A resistance song, starked poems,
In ink, they fight against what's wrong.
Line by line, a protest unfurls,
Against the discord of war's cruel swirls.
Antiwar Poetry, a defiant brigade,
Loud stanzas, a global peace campaign.
Amidst the chaos, the verses stand,
A testament to peace, letter after letter.
Each anti-war poem, a hope to sow,
In hearts and minds of people.
So let the lines speak, about freedoms,

About innocent children and the brightness of dawn.
Let your pen write about justice and humanity
And say,
War's toll, we'll no longer pay.
©® TAGHRID BOU MERHI
LEBANON/ BRAZIL
*****

SHIKDAR MOHAMMED KIBRIAH
(Bangladesh)
TITLE: A PUPPET WORLD

Roaring in the sky!
Bombing on the land!!
The Arabians viewing thunders
And hearing its roaring
Just like a natural occurrence.
Passing peaceful days
With normal activities
As if normal randomly bomb-blast
At Ghaza.
Firing hospitals, schools, homes
Mosques and public buildings.
Brutally killing children, women
And, innocent unarmed people!
Running absolutely a genocide!
Seems all of the global leaders
Enjoying Hollywood war movie
As the Arabian enjoy Arabian nights!
Composed a human tragedy
By the western mastermind
Truly one eyed loud speaker
Of human rights and world peace,
Patronize the barbaric occupation.
What a shame! What a tragedy!
Still sleeping the puppet world
In air condition,
Enjoying Arabian nights, and
Dreaming for a fairytale solution

***

SAJID HUSSAIN
(Pakistan)
< teacherimsb@gmail.com >

LOVE, PEACE AND HUMANITY (2)

Freshness from some pulses for humanity,
Wins heart of universe with worthiness ,
The blinks of the autumnal days get rest,
When courtesy of soul sparks on sympathy,
Harmonic waves of love ripple a glow,
Catching headlong vigor of sheer peace ,
Light of peace on wizard way flights with love,
When devastating storm of war whirls around life's horizon,
The crumbling ashes of thundering hate,
Will never awake on zone of love,
The humanity shines
for pale leaves of breath,
Under the guidance of love and peace,
Whenever roaring ocean of hate and war,
Springs up in any moment on the sea of life,
For peace the ghost of hostility disappears soon,
The fragrance of peace with drops of love,
Dissipates hissing matters of life like smoke,
Its silver gleam sparks sick hearts ,
Saps the nectar of wither flowers with humane dew,
To crush down the urge of severe cold,
Beams of new dawn rise after every dark night,
Having light and warmth of love and peace.

***

FATIMA USMAN(Pakistan)

"WAR AGAINST WAR"

*I witnessed
A child in turmoil,
desperately seeking his mother,
The wind carried whispers of his mother's essence Longing to reach,
extending a heart's helping hand,
But the gunpowder's grasp muted the breeze's lament
The child's screams echoed,
a desperate call to his mother,
The Waves of his voice yearning for aid, But explosions shackled
the very essence of sound..
Blood spilled,
a poignant testimony to despair Corpses, Silent witnesses
strewn across the desolation
The sky wept,
clouds heavy with sorrow,
The earth cried out,
burdened by the weight of agony,
Humanity gasped its last breath.
I Saw
A powerful spectacle unfolding,
a tragedy of epic proportions,
Mountains wept as*

their ancient stoicism crumbling,
Rivers pleaded for mercy,
the lifelines of despair Humanity,
a fading heartbeat,
nearing its final throes.
I saw
Within the four walls,
a facade of normalcy
Eating while news aired on TV,
a surreal detachment,
Similar hunger within their hungry homes,
a cruel irony
And the powerful knew,
a callous acknowledgment
"Better them than Us,"
They continued to fill
their mouths with spoons,
oblivious Walls wept,
bearing silent witness to the charade, Windows cried out,
framing the tragedy in their panes, Humanity was dying,
its pulse weakening.
I witnessed
The powerful's pockets growing lighter,
a ruthless calculus
Crushing the weak,
a heartless
Thinking, "If the weak remain hungry,
my pocket will stay full, so
This spectacle must continue.."
A cruel resolve I'm watching,
a sigh escapes, laden with despair,
The weak world is ending,

a heartrending finale
Tears of blood absorbing within,
a poignant metaphor
The earth turns barren,
a desolate landscape
Sky's tears start to dry,
hope evaporating,
Mountains restlessly
abandon their places,
a world unhinged,
Humanity is dying,
a mournful requiem
The universe readies itself,
a solemn prelude
For the war against the war...

* * *

JASNA GUJIC
YOU

You who have never
crossed the boundaries of the dream
teach me to shout
from mountain tops
at the end of the day
teach me to open my hands
clenched in fists
and do not be gentle
like those
who give kisses to everyone,
without tenderness.

Do not be false,
latent and arrogant,
be yourself all the way,
be the one
who does not leave his heart
in himself
but gives it to beat
in someone else's chest.
And only then
will I let you
into the caves of my loneliness,
wilderness and silence,
too silent.
I will allow you
to cross the boundaries
of all limitationsand enter my heart of infinity
* * *

YOUR NAME

Your name is inscribed somewhere
ahead of all my scratch of wanderings
and all my prayers.
You are standing astonished
on the path of my life
and I am dancing in the silence
in a white gown with a flower
in my hair beside you.
And I knew,
you are the one
who gave the color
to the gray sad eyes.
Your name is inscribed somewhere
in some book of life

that sounds so vital
leaving just a kiss behind.
Indelible.
Let's run away.
The carriages are waiting for us.
* * *

FEAR

I'm standing naked
in front of my own fear.
Only him and me
in front of the mirror of life.
And I'm watching him
with wide eyes opened
and I'm asking him,
is he afraid of my ego
and my crazy desire to win.
He looks silently at me,
my fear,
indifferent, without a blink of eye
without a heart,
and no hugs.
But now I feel like I'm prevailing,
crossing all obstacles of self-pity,
and the curses of the evil men in black.
And I feel my big fear shrinking
as I walk on my toes,
over-running years of nonsense.
And I was born again
in the glare of the Universe,
free of burdens of the life
free to fly, somewhere
where no one can touch

my wings of the dreamer
** * **

TONIGHT

Tonight
I could only write about you
long,
tender and incessantly,
without reason,
without blinking,
No regrets.
Just like my heart
Without programs,
Without schemes,
no combination.
Because you are,
of course,
gentle
and lazy,
but as if i knew everything about you
and you around,
as if it had always belonged to those
hands,
eyes,
Hugs.
Tonight
I could only write about you
and I touch the stars
with my hands
because you gave me your shine
THE MOMENT
At my fingertips,
I feel

the touch of your soul
wrapped in my colorful scarf
fluttering through the summer hot air.
And I'm smiling in the silence.
From far away the scent of sea
you brought to me
foaming in my eyes
and the sound of the waves
crowned in blue.
And I wish to capture
just that moment
and your step
with your smile of longing
As you walk along
the sunny side of the street.
All Rights Reserved@Jasna Gugic

* * *

KAMTA PERSAD(India)
<kamtaps@yahoo.com> wrote:

There is a wicked war a raging
In Ukraine, Gaza , guns blazing.
hot shrapnel through youthful human flesh
untimely death.
paper mask falls away ,to reveal
the contorted masque of human agony ,death
when will they ever learn?
Missed?
we will build a better device tomorrow
to burn and and incinerate human flesh
as young men fall like bowling pins ,all in a row
the other side celebrates,, makes videos on Utube
war is now a spectator sport
we celebrate human death, we do.
Hiroshima and Nagasaki soon?
they will never learn.

***

YOUSUF KHALID (Pakistan)

ہوا شکوہ کناں ہے

مری سانسوں میں اتری خوشبوئیں

اور سبزہ گل سے مزین کوہساروں،

بہتے چشموں،گنگناتی آبشاروں کی جبیں کو چومتا

سرشار ہوتا یہ مرا بھیگا ہوا پیکر

مری رفتار

میرا موسموں کے ساتھ ہر لمحہ بدلتا پیرہن

اور خوشنما پھولوں، پرندوں، ننھے بچوں،

اور گہری نیند میں سوئی ہوئی

الہڑ جواں شہزادیوں اور شہ زادوں کے حسیں خوابوں میں

ہر دم شبنمی احساس سے لبریز

لاکھوں خواہشیں تقسیم کرتا،

شام کی گہری اداسی میں حسیں یادوں کو اذنِ گفتگو دیتا،

نئی صبح کے اجلے منظروں میں

خواب کی تعبیر کے امکان رکھتا،

دلنشیں کردار ——————————— اتنا مضمحل کیوں ہے؟

زمیں زادے مرے اس دلنشیں کردار سے اب بد گماں کیوں ہیں

یہ آخر کس لیے؟

بگڑے ہوئے حالات کی زد میں ہے

آخر کون ہے وہ؟

جس نے مجھ سے خوشبوئیں لے کر مجھے بارود کی بو

بے حسی کی گرد میں لپٹا ہوا

ماحول بخشا ہے

مرے اجلے بدن کو کس نے میلا کر دیا ہے ؟
***

خدشات کی آنکھ میں پلتی ہوئی کہانی

ویران راستے سیاہی مائل راکھ سے اٹے پڑے ہیں
درختوں کی بے برگ شاخوں میں نمی نام کو باقی نہیں
جہاں سبزہ تھا وہاں بے نور بے جان بھربھری مٹی کے ڈھیر لگے ہیں
اپنی شان و شوکت پہ اتراتی آسماں کو چھوتی عمارتیں
ہیبت ناک کھنڈرات کا منظر پیش کر رہی ہیں
ہر طرف جانوروں ، انسانوں اور پرندوں کی باقیات پڑی ہیں
ہوا میں تابکاری کی زہر ناکی بھری ہوئی ہے
جا بجا تاریخ، تہذیب اور تمدن کے بد ہیئت ڈھانچے بکھرے پڑے ہیں
وسیع و عریض تہہ خانوں میں جمع کیا ہوا رزق اور آکسیجن سے بھری
ٹینکیوں نے
جنوں آمیز رعونت کی سانسیں ابھی تک بحال رکھی ہوئی ہیں
ایک خوش گمانی
مصنوعی سانسوں کے سہارے زندگی گزارنے والوں کو تسلیاں دینے میں
مصروف ہے
کہ زندگی پھر سے ویرانوں کو آباد کرے گی
نئی سحر طلوع ہو گی
مگر مسلسل کم ہوتے ہوئے رزق اور آکسیجن کی کمی نے
موت کا خوف اور مایوسی بڑھا دی ہے
اور دھرتی کی بحالی کے امکانات محدود کر دیے ہیں
فتح اور شکست کے کوئی معنی نہیں رہے
دھرتی کی چھاتی پر اپنی عظمت ،اپنی ہیبت اور اپنی حکمرانی کا جھنڈا
لہرانے والے
سوئے فلک دیکھ رہے ہیں
کہ کہیں سے زندگی کے بانجھ پن کے لیے آبِ حیات اترے
سماوی نعمتوں کا نزول ہو
سبز و گل کی حکمرانی ہو
پرندے پھر سے چہچہانے لگ جائیں
احساسِ زیاں کی کوکھ سے پھر کوئی امید کی کونپل پھوٹے
یوسف خالد

***

SARWAT ZAHRA (Pakistan)

WONDERLAND

Before the collar was the neck,
And before the neck, one upon one,
The vertebrae's nested ascent.

Before pen and ink, the finger,
And before the finger, its reaching nerves.
Before sounds, the mouth, this tongue enlivened
By an intricate tatting.
When invisible stays pulled the tent of the eye's
Full whiteness round, the pupil formed
And spectacle followed. But even before
The eye took shape, eons of travel,
Time's dark abyss.
Behold this Journey!
And before the first steps
An intention moved—
You in my heart . . . primordial longing,
Issuing first from the stench of caves,
My helix scratched on their walls . . .
And before the before
And before once more—
What first divide?

* * *

حیرت کدہ

گریباں سے پہلے یہ گردن،
تو گردن سے پہلے؟
مہربان مہروں کی خود پر چڑھائی
قلم روشنائی سے پہلے یہ انگلی
تو انگلی سے پہلے رگوں کی ترائی
صداوں سے پہلے دہن ،یہ زباں
اور ان سے بھی پہلے --
یہ عصبی کڑھائی
تماشے سے پہلے یہ پتلی
سفیدی کی عریانطنابیں
تو اس سے بھی پہلے
اندھیری لکیروں کی کھائی
سفر !
تجھ سے پہلے قدم
اور اس سے بھی پہلے
ارادوں کی ہیئت کذائی
مرے دل میں تُوتیری خواہش
تری خواہشوں سے بھی پہلے
گپھاوں کا باسی تنفس
مرے جینیاتی نظاموں کی پہلی لکھائی
تو پہلے سے،
پہلے سے
پہلے کی کیسی جدائی؟
* * *

TIME NEEDS SLEEP

When night's dew drenches the stairs
And arches of churches, of synagogues, mosques,

A shredded blanket covers the beggar
Asleep in the street.
Desires cast upon water all night
Have turned the oceans to oil.
Hands that fed the park's fishes
Have returned to their jobs.
Naked feet that whispered together
While couples on beaches counted waves
Now only meet in their beds.
Seagulls' wings that quilled clear breezes
Now must learn to write with smoke.
The tottering morning,
Arm-in-arm with the time-worn sun,
Staggers, groggy, away.

***

وقت کو سو جانا چاہیے

عبادت گاہ کی سیڑھیاں اور محرابیں
رات بھر کے کہر سے گیلی ہو گئیں
سڑک پہ سوئے فقیر نے
اپنے پھٹے ہوئے کمبل سے بدن لپیٹ لیا
پانی کی سطح پہ رکھی ہوئی خواہشوں سے
رات بھر اتنا تیل رستا رہا
کہ سمندر کثیف ہوگیا

کنارے پر بیٹھ کر مچھلیوں کو
دانہ ڈالنے والے ہاتھ
اپنے اپنے کاموں پر جا چکے
ریت پر بیٹھ کر سرگوشیاں کرتے ننگے پیر
لہروں کے حساب میں مصروف جوڑے
صرف بستروں میں ملاقات کا وقت نکال سکیں گے

مرغابیوں اور کبوتروں کے اجلے پروں پر ہوا

دھوئیں سے نقش نگاری سیکھ رہی ہے

آفتابِ وقت

صبح کے پہلو بہ پہلو

نیند میں جھومتا

ڈگمگاتا

چلا جا رہا ہے

***

THE QUEEN OF THE INTERNET

On your throne of clouds, O Queen of Dreams,
How long will your silken fingertips
Stitch hope on our palms?
Beauty rises in your brilliant courtyard—
Flashing pictures, dreamy illusions, red velvet mites,
And full ripe grapes to make us drunk.
Yet even here, from a cistern brimming
With loneliness, a drop splashes out.
In a crowded café you flash bright signs:
Love and desire—burning lips, laughter and sobs.
But everything here is just half-true, a moment's façade.
You'll drown in your clouds,
O Queen of Dreams!
In crowded chat rooms, icy hearts
Devour emotions, gnaw raw souls,
Choking behind their human masks.
Loneliness does its colorful dance on burning words.
How long will you fan their dying embers?
O Queen of Dreams on your throne of clouds,
Thirst will finally ask for rain.

***

انٹرنیٹ استھان کی ملکہ

انٹرنیٹ استھان پہ بیٹھی خواب کی ملکہ !
مخمل سی پوروں سے کتنے روز بنو گی؟
خواب کی ریکھا
رنگ رنگیلے بیر بہوٹی جیسے لفظوں کی انگنائی
جلتی بجھتی تصویروں کی خواب سرائی
ثابت انگوروں کے دانوں جیسی
دنیا کی یہ ہوش ربائی
تنہائی کی گاگر سے پھر لمحہ چھلکا
انٹرنیٹ استھان پہ بیٹھی خواب کی ملکہ !
دور کسی کیفے میں بیٹھے
خواہش اور محبت کے یہ اجلے سائن
یہ جلتے ہونٹوں کے خط،
یہ ہنسنا رونا
سب کچھ آدھا سچ ہے
آدھے سچ میں ڈوب مرو گی
گور کھدھندا بس اک پل کا
انٹرنیٹ استھان پہ بیٹھی خواب کی ملکہ !
چیٹنگ روم میں
سرد دلوں کے رش میں گھٹتی سانسیں
انسانوں کے چہرے پہنے
جذبے کھائیں روح چبائیں
تنہائی کے روپ رنگیلے رقص دکھائیں
حرفوں کے بجھتے انگارے
کتنے دن تک اور چنو گی؟
پیاس تو مانگے رستہ جل کا
انٹرنیٹ استھان پہ بیٹھی خواب کی ملکہ !

***

SAJJAD AZHER(PAKISTAN)

من کی آشا

(غزہ پر اسرائیلی حملوں کے پس منظر میں

کیا ایسا نہیں ہوسکتا کہ ہم گھروں کی حفاظت کے لیے

پھر سے کتے پال لیں کتے کی وفاداری کی گواہ صدیاں ہیں اور

غاروں کی

وہ تاریک کوٹھریاں ہیں

جہاں انسان نے اپنا خوفزدہ ماضی گزارا تھا گھروں کے ساتھ اگر

سرحدیں بھی

کتوں کے حوالے کر دی جائیں تو آئے روز کی گولیوں سے

بے گناہ انسان مرنا بند ہو جائیں کیونکہ

امن کی امید اب کتوں سے ہی رہ گئی ہے

لنڈی کوتل کی لالٹین

ہاتھوں میں کاغذ کی ڈگریاں تھامے ہم نے کتنے ہی

دفتروں کے پتے ازبر کر لیے مگر نوکری نہیں

ملی

لنڈی کوتل کی لائینوں کی روشنی میں پڑھتے

پڑھتے ہماری بینائی تو سلامت رہ گئی مگر

سونگھنے کی حس کو

لالٹینوں میں جلنے والے تیل نے متاثر کیا جس
سے ہماری سوچنے کی حس کم اور سونگھنے کی
تیز ہوگئی
اس زمانے میں
لنڈی کوتل سے آگے
زمینیں آگ اگل رہی تھیں
لنڈی کوتل میں بھی اب جرمنی کی لالٹینوں کی
جگہ امریکی بندوقوں کی دُکانیں کھل گئی تھیں
جنہیں چلانے کی ڈگریاں
مدرسوں سے ملتی تھیں
نوکری کے لیے ہماری ڈگری تو کام نہیں آئی البتہ
آگ سونگھنے کی صلاحیت ہمیں اخباروں میں لے
گئی
جہاں باقی زندگی ہم نے
آگ اگلتی سُرخیاں نکالنے میں گزار دی

SIDRA SAHAR IMRAN(Pakistan)

P

oet, writer, essayist, fictionist, novelist and play/script writer Sidra Sahar Imran hails from Karachi, Pakistan. She was born on August 8, 1986 in a very traditional family. She got her early education in Karachi. She got her master degree in Urdu literature from University of Karachi. From the very childhood she fall in love with words and books and that love transformed her to one of most of powerful and rebellious voices of contemporary Urdu Literature. She started writing from very childhood. She wrote poetry, fiction, novels, articles, features and columns. Her work has been published in numerous Urdu Journals and magazines of Pakistan and India. She wrote novels for commercial digests too. Her books Moat Ki Rehearsal (Translated into English Death's Rehearsals)and Hum Gunah ka Istahara Hein (We: The Metaphors of Sin) got huge applauds from the critics and readers. She is also a scripts and play writer and writes for different TV Channels of Pakistan. Her most popular Play Jalan aired from AryDigital made headlines one social media and Print media. Her Interview about Jalan Controversy .She Also wrote a hit drama Amrat or Maya(Express Entertainment)and Mujhe Pyaar Hua Tha(Arydigital)

***

چیخ کے نام پر ایک سڑک

ہمیں اپنے شہر کی رحلوں میں اتارو
ہمارے داغ پڑھو
دیکھو ہمارے پاؤں اپنے تعاقب میں مڑ گئے
ہم اپنی تلاش کی سڑکوں پر
وہ کھوئے ہوئے آثار بن گئے
جہاں زندگی کے بے جان بت
مل رہے ہیں
ہمیں عجائب گھروں میں آواز دو
ڈھونڈو ہماری آنکھیں
!!شاید تمہارے ملبے میں دب گئی ہیں

ایک قبر کا جنم دن

آزادی ایک نظم تھی
جو اجتماعی آبروریزی کے ہاتھوں
اس عورت کی قبر میں دفنادی گئ
جس کا بیٹا
تقسیم ہند کے میلے میں بچھڑ گیا تھا
عورت کو یاد نہیں
کتنے مرد اس کے ہونٹوں کا ناپ اٹھائے
قومی ترانے کا ورد کرتے
تماشاگاہوں میں جھومتے تھے
اور ہم رقص کرنے کے جرم میں
اپنے ہاتھ پیر گنوائے
مسجد کی آخری صفوں میں
نمازیوں کی جوتیاں سنبھالتے
وطن کی سلامیاں اکھٹی کرتے
اپنے ٹوٹے ہوئے گھروں کی
دیواریں بنتے رہے

ہماری آنکھوں کی تتلیاں

خاکی موسموں کا زہر کھا گیا

گیلے کاغذ کی کشتیوں میں

ہماری بستیوں کا کاٹھ کباڑ لاد دے

عقابوں کی اندھی ٹولیاں

برگد کے بوڑھے پیڑ پر

اس کا پچھتر ہواں جنم دن مناتے ہوئے

اجاڑ ماں سے کہہ رہی ہیں

رقص کر

رقص کر اس سے پہلے کہ تیرے یوسف کی

دو گز زمین بچانے کے لیے

ہم اس کی ہڈیوں سے ہاتھ سینکیں

اس کی کھال سے جیکٹیں بنا کر

خودکشی کی فیکٹریوں پر وار آئیں

رقص کر۔۔

***

ایک یادگاری ٹکٹ

اس موسم کا کوئی نام رکھا جائے

جب مٹی کے تمام درختوں سے

گہرے رنگ کی قبریں پھوٹ رہی ہوں

اور لوگ ایک دوسرے میں

اپنا آپ ڈھونڈتے پھریں

کوئی بولے

دیکھو میرے پاؤں غائب ہیں

کوئی قہقہہ لکھنا سیکھ رہا ہو

کسی کے ہاتھ پر لکیریں آنکھ مچولی کھیلتی ہوں

کوئی اپنی آنکھیں گندی نالیوں میں

تلاشنا ہو
تم زور سے چیخو
" یہ دیواریں مجھے اپاہج نہیں کر سکتیں "
اور میں اپنی آواز کی کترنوں سے
ایک پرچم بناؤں
جو ہمارے جسموں پر لپٹا جائے
اس پر لکھوں
" خاموشی کا ایک مطلب گالی بھی ہوتا ہے "

پھولوں کی ہار بیڑیوں میں کیسے بدلتے ہیں
چپ کی تھالی میں
ہاں کا جبری رنگ پھینکتے ہوئے
میں عزت کی سیاہ چادر میں
جذب ہوگئی
میری ڈور تھامنے والے کی شکل کیسی ہے
مجھ کیا مطلب
وہ اپنی سوچ کے گندے جوہڑ میں
عورت پن کی مچھلیاں شکار کرتے ہوئے
مجھ پر دیوانہ وار ہنستا ہے
میرے آنسو
نلکے کے پانی سے بھی ہلکے ہیں
ایک میلا کچیلا دل
دھونے کے کام بھی نہیں آ سکتے
میرے پاؤں میں ان گنت لکیریں ہیں
مگر میں اپنی پیشانی کا جال
ختم نہیں کر سکتی
میں غیرت کی گٹھری میں بندھی ہوئی

ناجائز عورت ہوں
میرا مرد نہیں جانتا
کہ میرا دل کسی اور سے بیاہا ہوا ہے

***

نمک حرام زندگی

ہم نے روٹی نہیں
آگ چرائی
ہم نے پانی نہیں
پتھر ابالے
ہم نے جوتے نہیں
سڑکیں پہنیں
ہم نے پرندے نہیں
آنکھیں قید کیں
ہم نے زیورات نہیں
زنجیریں جمع کی
ہم نے پھول نہیں
زخم کاڑھے
یم نے بارش کی دعاؤں میں
ہتھیلیاں گروی رکھیں
ہم نے مکانوں کے بھیس میں
قبروں کی تراش خراش کی
ہم نے آسماں پر اپنے آنسو بوکر
بارشیں کاشت کیں
اور عمر بھر زندگی سے
نمک مانگتے رہے

***

پانی دریا کو ایک قتل معاف کر سکتا ہے؟

ریل کی پٹریوں پر ہماری خیریت
مشکوک ہو کر گر پڑی ہے
ہواؤں نے ہم سے راستہ چھپانے سے پہلے
پرندوں کو درخت واپس نہیں کیے
پتھروں کو ہمارے گھر کا پتہ
ایک ایسی دیوار نے دیا
جس میں محبت چنی گئی تھی
گلیوں میں تہمتیں پھینکی جا رہی ہیں
اور .....
ٹیلی فونک کھڑکیوں میں ہماری بدنامیاں
کئی راتیں پھلانگ چکیں
سورج اپنے قبیلے میں
ہماری جبری گم شدگی کا اعلان کرتا پھر رہا ہے
روشنی ہمارے زائچوں سے
بہت دور نکل گئی
ہمیں تاریکیوں کو خط بھیجنے دو
وگرنہ ......
موم بتیاں ہماری قبروں پر
احتجاج کرنے نہیں آئیں گی
ہم ہجوم کے پیروں میں مسلے ہوئے گلاب ہیں
ہم اپنے دل کی بستیوں سے
دھتکارے ہوئے لوگ
ہماری آنکھیں اپنے جرگوں میں
ان تصویروں پر کاروکاری کا الزام لگاتی رہیں
جو کسی مصور سے مکمل نہیں ہوسکیں
ہمارے پیروں نے
ہمیں تمہارے شہر جانے سے روک دیا

کوئی جنم دن پر خودکشی بھی کرتا ہے؟
ہم اپنے بازوؤں کی صلیب پر
اس انکار کی طرح لٹکے رہے
جس کے فرقے میں دوگز زمین بھی نہیں ملتی
ہمیں پتھروں کے مول بیچا گیا
ہماری ہتھیلیوں سے
دعائیں تک اکھیڑی گئیں
سرد کانوں میں وہ شور پھونکا گیا
جو کسی کو بھی گستاخی کے نام پر
مار سکتا ہے
ہماری سانسیں سونگھ کر بتاؤ
خدا ہمیں پہچانتا ہے یانہیں؟

م سے موت

اپنے جوتوں سے پاؤں اتارو
اور محسوس کرو
لاپتہ ہونے کا دکھ
بغیر کھڑکی کے مکاں بناؤ
اور سوچو...
کیا تمہیں قبر سے محبت ہوئی؟
شہر کے کانوں میں جاکر زور سے
اپنا نام پکارو
کوئی نہ آئے تو سمجھو
دوگز زمین کا انعام نکل آیا ہے
جشن مناؤ..
گاؤں کی مسجدوں میں بھوکے بچے
من و سلویٰ کے سبق پر
اٹکے ہوئے تھے!!

فلسطین کے لئے

ہنسی کیا ہوتی ہے
ہمیں کیا معلوم
ہم نے تو گولیوں کی تڑ تڑ اہٹ میں
آنکھیں کھولیں
ہمیں کیا معلوم
گلابوں کی خوشبو کیا ہے
ہم نے تو بچپن سے لاشیں سونگھ کر
آنسوؤں کے کاروبار کئے
زخم ہمارے گھر کی کھیتی ہیں
ہم پیروں میں موت پہن کر
گھومتے ہیں
اور زندگی ہمارے ہاتھوں میں
دبے کنکروں جیسی ہے
کاش
ہم ان کنکروں کی مدد سے
دنیا کے سارے قابض فوجیوں کو
موت کے شناختی کارڈ بانٹ سکتے

میرے بستے میں
ایک کتاب ہے
اس کتاب میں
ب سے بم
کہیں نہیں لکھا
تمہیں وہ کتابیں
کس نے دیں
جس نے تمہیں

ق سے قتل سکھایا

فوجی انکل
آپ نے میرے ماں باپ کو مار دیا
حالانکہ
وہ آپ کے بیٹوں سے بھی
اتنا ہی پیار کرتے تھے
جتنا مجھ سے
پھر آپ نے میرے بہن بھائیوں سے کہا
بھاگو
بہت تیز بھاگو
اور قہقہے لگاتے ہوئے فائر کئے
ٹھاہ ٹھاہ ٹھاہ
فوجی انکل
آپ کی پستول میں ایک گولی باقی ہے
آپ مجھے بھی مار سکتے ہیں

میں نے مٹی سے
ایک فاختہ بناکر
خدا کے پاس بھیجی ہے
فاختہ
خدا سے
زیتون کی شاخ لے کر آئے گی
میں یہ زیتون
اپنی مٹی میں اگاؤں گا
اور
خدا سے کہوں گا
اس زمین پر سرخ رنگ

حرام کر دے

***

AMJAD BABAR

(PAKISTAN)

<amjadbabur@gmail.com>

ہمیں جنگ کرنی ہے

ہم جنگ کریں گے

غربت

ناخواندگی کے فرقوں

غیر مناسب سماجی رویوں

استحصالی قوتوں کے خلاف

یقیناً ہمارے ناخن گھس جائیں گے

لیکن

ہمارے خون سے

نئے دن کا سورج طلوع ہو گا

ہم جنگ کرتے رہیں گے

کمزور لوگوں کے حقوق کی خاطر

افراد میں

انسانیت کی تبلیغ

زندگی میں امن کی روح پھونکنے کے لیے

ہمیں جنگ کرنی ہو گی

اِس سے پہلے کہ

تاریکی کے پنجے

زمین کے معصوم چہروں کو نوچ لیں
پرندوں، جانوروں کا شکار کریں
تنور سے روٹی کے جلنے کی بُو آئے
اور ہمارے خوابوں کا کفن میلا ہو جائے

***

OTTERI SILVA KUMAR

وہ گناہ

زخمی اور نالی

...روح کے خون سے گناہوں کی تجدید نہیں ہوتی

میں نہیں جانتا

پرانے گناہ

...صرف ایک چیز رہ گئی ہے

...البتہ

اس روح کا خون

...آنسو

ان گناہوں سے

اسے غائب نہیں کہا جا سکتا

...دوبارہ ...دوبارہ

مرنا

پرانے گناہ

...کرتے رہو

What's up : 9840326848 چنئی - *600012*

***

ZAREEN AKHTAR
<zareen.akhtar1972@gmail.com>

جنگ کیوں ہوکر رہے گی؟

خون کیوں بہہ کر رہے گا؟

زمیں بانجھ ہے کیا؟

یا سیم و تھر کا شکار؟

یہ وہ دور تو نہیں کہ زمیں کو بھینٹ چاہیے؟

یا اب بھی وہی دور ہے؟

نہیں وہ تو دور جاہلیت میں ہوتا تھا ۔

اب تو انساں مہذب ہوگیا ہے ۔

زمیں کب خون کی بھینٹ مانگتی ہے؟

تو کیا تلواریں خون کی پیاسی ہیں؟

یہ کوئی تلواروں کا دور ہے

اب تمدن بدل چکا ہے ۔

تمدن کی تاریخ تہذیب پر بھاری ہے

سائنس تہذیب کی پیش رو ہے؟

یا

شہہ س

وار؟

یا

قاتل؟

یا انسان؟

خواہ وہ یہودی ہو یا مسلمان.
انسان کہلانے کا مستحق نہیں
لیکن جب بساط بچھتی ہے تو دونوں طرف
پیادے ہی کام آتے ہیں
پیارے ہی جاتے ہیں ۔

***

SHAHZAD DEEP (Pakistan)

جہاں زرخیز مٹی میں گلِ لالہ اُگانے ہوں

شہزاد دیپ جھنگ

جہاں بچوں نے روٹھے تتلیاں، جگنو منانے ہوں

جہاں پہ پھول سے معصوم چہرے مسکرانے ہوں

جہاں پہ مور ، چڑیا اور بلبل چہچہانے ہوں

جہاں کی وادیوں میں کہکشاں، سے رہ بنانے ہوں

جہاں سنسان اُجڑے دل کے آنگن پھر بسانے ہوں

جہاں مقصود ہو کہ آشیاں آباد کرنے ہیں

جہاں ایسا گُماں ہو کہ یہاں قُدسی اُترنے ہیں

جہاں افلاک کی مانند تارے آ بکھرنے ہیں

جہاں آ کے بہاروں نے گلابی رنگ بھرنے ہیں

وہاں پھر آگ کے دریا بہائے تو نہیں جاتے

وہاں بارود کے شعلے گرائے تو نہیں جاتے

، وہاں کی مسجدیں ،مندر ،کلیسے ،گُردوارے

درسگاہیں اور شفا خانے

مٹائے تو نہیں جاتے

وہاں کے بے گناہ شہری بہت ارزاں سمجھ کے

خوب کاٹے اور اڑائے تو نہیں جاتے

وہاں پہ کشت و خون اور دھویں کے رو سیاہ بادل اٹھائے تو نہیں

جاتے

وہاں جنگ و جَدَل کے حشر پرور آتشی میلے

سجائے تو نہیں جاتے

جہاں زرخیز مٹی میں گلِ لالہ اُگانے ہوں

جہاں بچوں نے روٹھے تتلیاں ، جگنو منانے ہوں

شہزاد دیپ جھنگ

***

SOME MORE POEMS
BY: FRANCESCO FAVETTA (ITALY)

The Poet Francesco Favetta was born in Sicily in Sciacca, he has always loved poetry, writing verses, but above all culture, true culture, food for the soul! So far he has written more than 4000 poems, he also writes philosophical reflections and thoughts.

In 2018, he was awarded and awarded by the Academy of Sicily Academician of Sicily.

EVERY SILENCE IS PEACE!

*Like the sun this heart burns
and every breath it is a powerful wind
that always breaks out
in the trials of life and
in truth it is never extinguished.
How many times has it been imposing
desert swept away by fury of warrior love
remained standing before the bitter songs to daily indifferences.
Without words
then the infinite thirst has been quenched and into the dark nights
every silence has become really loved sleep
absolute rest and Inner Peace.*

IN THIS SILENT HOUR

*It's already evening and the dim light
over the horizon gives way at first dark.
The song of the night he's already
knocking and the silence flies among the
darkness and in every breath.
And who knows how many lives they fall asleep
in this silent hour in beloved dreams
and inside the sleepless nig*

hts.

THE SONG OF LOVE

It is within time the song of love
does not change
doesn't give in it is always on in memories
in the moments and in the eyes.
It's like this everywhere laughs in a grateful voice
the song of love is strong
it is a profound mystery remained rock
he is blessed divine feeling and enchantment in the heart

IN THE DARK NIGHT OF PEACE

We will see
how it will go to finish in this pilgrimage
without return so desperate
because it's not easy travel together
with the truth and to the heart around the world
in the desert in the doubts of life and in silence
remained motionless in the dark night of Peace killed by
man.

LIFE !

Life tell me how many times
have you come near the dark
and then from the sudden jousts
your voice still sang without stopping in the wind
and when you swallow poisons
you are always reborn again.
Precious life beautiful portrait sleepless
awakening in the heart
you my life tree with deep roots
often on your lips the song of love
it was the most beautiful music.

Life without skin next to your wounds
my every smile was the blood response
mine getting bigger the arduous happy song
the divine Comedy that faithful warrior heart of mine.
My life how many more steps within this time
in the folds of the days along the journey of Faith
in this sea that never stops in the routes of the
beloved song.

MAHJOOR BADAR

(PAKISTAN)

<mahjoorbadar@gmail.com>

نظمیہ

ہمیں اب نظم نہیں لکھنا چائیے

مہجور بدر

ہمیں ہوا کے بہتی آنسوؤں کو

پرندوں کے ہجرتوں کو

جھیلوں کے مچھلیوں کو

آسمان کی نیلگوں چادر کو

استعارہ بنانے کی ضروت نہیں

!!! ہمیں اب نظم نہیں لکھنا چائیے

***

ARİF BUZOVNALI

(AZERBAİJAN)

.A World Famous Poet

:An Article by
Mesme Ismayilova

A

zerbaijani literature has an ancient history developing way. And this literature is the irreplaceable, valuable national-cultural wealth of Azerbaijani people. Azerbaijani literature played an important role in the formation of the country as an independence state and in the social-developing of the people.

Azerbaijani people gave the world literature the greatest geniuses. Such as Nizami Ganjevi, Imamaddin Nasimi, Muhammad Fizuli,Shah Ismayil Khatai, Mirza Fatali Akhundov, Jalil Mammadquluzade,Mirza Alakbar Sabir, Samad Vurgun, Rasul Rza, and others,who lived and created for people and the world. And nowadays, there are many creative persons, who continuous their creation. One of them is Arif Rahman Aliyev.

Arif Aliyev was born September 6,in 1972, in Azerbaijan,in the countryside of Buzovna in Baku.That is why, he took the penname Arif Buzovnali.

He went to the military service, and then completed his serving in the Soviet Army, in 1992. Althgough, he entered to the Azerbaijan State Pedagogical University in 1993, but he voluntarily went to the Karabakh battle-front before starting his education and fought in the "Volunteer Battalion" named after Azizbekov, until the ceasefire

(1 May, 1994). The literary activity of Arif Buzovnaly dates back to his early years. His poem, which named " Imitation to Vahid", that didn't publish in the magazine "Pioneer" in 1987, as it didn't correspond to the concept of the magazine, but in 1991 the same poem was published on the newspaper "Azerbaijan ganjlari" ("Azerbaijani youngs"). He was a member of various literary mejlis (literary parties) acting in Baku and Absheron, including "Fuzuli" and "Majmaush-Shuara". Regularly appeared in the media and press, such as "Azerbaijan Ganjali", "Kaspi", "Iki Sahil", "Yol", "Olaylar", "Literaturnaya Gazeta", "Tek Sabir", "Nabz", "Shahriyar" and other newspapers, as well as magazines "Hikmet", "Kalam", "Ulduz", "Karvan", "Azerbaijan" with his literary works and articles on various theme during the period. He became the winner several times of the competition such as: International poetry "Sheri-tanz", held on in Tabriz, in 2003; Razavi International Poetry Festival in Urmia, in 2010; and he was the jury of Turkish-language Poetry Festival from 2011 till 2016. He participated in many scientific and literary conferences, which held in Azerbaijan, Turkey, Iran, Ukraine, Russia and was awarded various diplomas and awards. His poems have been translated into foreign languages and published on the press of different countries. He is the author of 7 literary books. His literary works took place in "Khazar tazkira (memoirs) ", "Hidden treasure", "All roads lead to Shusha, "Pearls from hidden treasures" and other anthologies and collections. He had translations from world literary from Omar Khayyam, Sergei Yesenin and Leyla Aliyeva."Khatai and Fizuli... Thoughts", "Nasimi at the review", "Forty Ghazals - Forty Explanations", " Chun ahsany teqvim (the name of scientific article, was taken from Nasimi's poems, and Nasimi took this line from Koran, and it means that humanity is the best of creation by Almighty)" and other researches were published in various press and books. He is a member of Azerbaijan Writers' Union from 2011; the chairman of Khazar Writers' Union from 2016; the chairman of

"Poetry Club" which established under the Khazar Creative Union from 2017; the chairman of Azerbaijan Writers' Union Commission under the name "Fizuli". Married, has two children.

Every time, when we talk about classic literature, we specifically note, that it is not impossible to read the works without feeling every line of couplets word by word.

Sometimes reader sits for hours not only over a Ghazal, but even over a verse. Of course, for the simple reader, this may be boring, but for word thinkers, this is may be great research.

Ghazal is a genre in which each couplet is free and connected only by a common spirit and technical parameters. For poets, who wants to show their talent in order to express deep meaning in a few words, the Ghazal was a real sphere of creation and it remains so today.

The main problem is not only to express the thought in Aruz (classical poetic weight in eastern poetry) in a verse, but to decorate it with artistic means of expression, to decorate it with the words, but to be able to give several thoughts.

Persian and Turkish verses, which had written in Aruz, have put a deep literary vestige than Arabic-aruz verses.Everybody knows, that art, literature, poetry haven't any borders. The reason of this is connoisseurs, creators from every corner of the world. And Azerbaijan is one of the popular countries from this point of view also.

Word predecessors from Azerbaijan are Nizami Ganjavi, Mahammad FizuliI made din Nasimi, recently Aliagha Vahid and nowadays Arif Buzovnali. All of them are creators of ghazal, and have their own styles. Nizami Ganjavi is famous with his "Where?","Without you"; Mahammad Fizuli :"You saw ,with the grief fire was grappled, my glad heart" ; " Having thousand grief I, which never will hide"; ImadeddinNasimi :"Two worlds fit in me,but I can't fit to this world";"Love is hard feeling, don't be flippand"; Aliagha Vahid :"If you would know, my pretty";"I wouldn't know,whose lovely beloved is this?".And nowadays Arif Buzovnali continues this style.

Arif's creativity is very colourful. He was activities as the member of different literary parties such as: "Fizuli";" Mejmeush shuare" which were activity in Baku and Absheron (Azerbaijan).

Also his literary works and different kinds of articles were published in journals and newspapers:"Azerbaijan genjleri"(Young's of Azerbaijani); "Yol"(Way);" Kaspi"(Caspi); "Olay-lar" (Events);"Edebiyyat qezeti" (Literary Newspaper)."Shahriyar"(Shahriar), "Azerbaijan", "Karvan"(Caravan) and other notable works.His literary works had been published an online poetry journals and anthologies. One of this journals is Our Poetry Archive (founder editor is Nilavro Nill Shoovro) and Poetic Galaxy ATUNIS.

(founder editor is Agron Shele; Albania)

He wrote many poems and gazelle.He wrote some of them without names,such as:

,Come, lovely angel, come, this is the day of your coming"

.This is the day of sharing your grieve, mourning with me

From my tears were redden the Hijri diary

.Leave the suffering , this is your resting day today

Was asked me, you said" may be, died he today"

It is your dad love off my sigh of sorrow,

Your tears would be flown for me tomorrow, d

on't think today,

Laugh above to me enough that, is your

laughing day today

Wipe my ill-fate love from the sorrow board also,

This is your day to wipe out of trace one by one,

Be forbearing, Arif, you will not die from trouble,

Your day of death, is the day that, the bud

.would take pity to you

Here the poet explains his feeling, his sorrow with angel and his the "death day

The next poem is about his "Love song" with his beloved. He tries to explain, that their song isn't as wailful song as other. He wrote, that their love song is full of with life and love…

"This isn't ours love song,
Ours wasn't so wailful,
Ours was crazy, was irascible,
.Ours wasn't boring, tiresome and long
This isn't ours love song,
Ours was sourish, but no sweet,
Words weren't so injuring,
Its regret wasn't so deep
This isn't ours love song,
Ours would have overrun, like the torrent,
It would scorch and burnt the Sun in the mornings,
.And would whip with the Moon in the evenings
This isn't ours love song,
Ours was piercing the ears and eyes,
Ours rhythm would break rhythm of hearts,
The voices would trickle down from the heart,
".This isn't ours love song

Arif Buzovnali wrote many poems and Ghazals. And the content of these literary works were always different from each other. One of his poems under the name "Clock" has philosophical meaning. The poet explained his thought "time and he" in this poem:

"Clock, which I hung on the wall, for morning
Hangs my faith from my words, every day
Revolving, rotating round my head, without stopping,
.And would hang a veil of ignorance on my eyes
Hands of this clock has sting me,
Sting me from the tongue, which telling the truth,

Sting me, from the hand holding a pen,
.This clock brought upon many troubles to me
That, I didn't feel the fortunate day,
From my sweet sleep, woke me up,
Was never afraid of something I in the world,
.Only this clock, has scared me
It may be my years have melted,
And was gone in a few minutes,
Catching from the hem, and said ? "don't go"
.Dragged me, and gone
The blind hour hands go to the same place,
I secretly pursued it, the thousand times.
?t narrowed my life, my day, but I
"Hanged it, from the widest wall

Arif Buzovnali took part at international poetry competitions. One of them is poetry compotition "Sheri-tenz"(couplets of poem) and won, which had hold in Tabriz; Razavi International Poetry Festival, which had been hold in Urmia, in 2003.Then twice, was judge at Tirkish language poetry Festival in Turkey. Arif also took part in many scientific and literary conferences, which held in Azerbaijan, Turkey, Iran, Ukraine, and Russia and was awarded various diplomas and awards. His poems have been translated into foreign languages and published in the press of different countries.
All these creations are proud for Azerbaijan and Azerbaijani people !

MESME ALIYULLA ISMAYILOVA
.Doc. Philology on Philosophy
.Azerbaijan State Pedagogical University